The ONE TALENT CHALLENGE
OVERCOMING INACTION AND FEAR

TONY LEE

www.revtonylee.com

Copyright © 2023 Rev. Tony Lee

All Rights Reserved

Scripture taken from the HOLY BIBLE, NEW INTERNATIONAL VERSION®. NIV®. Copyright © 1973, 1978, 1984 by International Bible Society

ISBN: 979-8-9895759-0-9 (paperback)

ISBN: 979-8-9895759-1-6 (e-book)

To my parents, Orlando Lee and Rev Nancy Lee, Ph.D,
who continue to challenge me to maximize
all of the talents God has given me.

Contents

Introduction vii

Chapter 1 The Gift of Trust 1

Chapter 2 The Talent Graveyard 7

Chapter 3 Trauma and Talents 13

Chapter 4 The Seasonal Nature of Talents 19

Chapter 5 Sermons In The Soil 27

Chapter 6 Dig It Up 33

Conclusion 39

Introduction

"Life is either a daring adventure or nothing at all."

– Helen Keller

Welcome to "**The One Talent Challenge: Overcoming Inaction and Fear**," a transformative journey through the parable of the talents, as told in Matthew 25:14-30. This book is designed to unearth the hidden treasures within this timeless story, inviting you to dig deeper into its profound lessons and apply them to your life.

In this parable, Jesus narrates the story of a master who, before going on a journey, entrusts his property to his servants according to their abilities. One receives five talents, another two, and the last, one talent. The first two servants multiply their talents, while the third, out of fear, buries his single talent. Upon the master's return, the first two are rewarded, but the third faces the master's displeasure for his inaction.

The Parable of the Talents is not just a story; it's a profound reflection of life's intricate dance with opportunity and the myriad ways we respond to it. At its core, it's about stewardship—of resources, of opportunities, and ultimately, of our own lives. The master, on his departure, entrusts his servants with his property, each according to their ability. The first two multiply what they are given, but the third, paralyzed by fear, buries his single talent, only to face his master's disappointment upon his return. It's a narrative that challenges the inertia born of fear and the complacency of the status quo.

As we explore the pages of this book, we will uncover the rich tapestry of trust the master weaves by entrusting his servants with his wealth. Each talent given is a testament to the master's belief in his servants' potential and their capacity to grow what they are given. Yet, in today's success-driven culture, the "one talent man" is often shadowed by negativity, his perceived inaction a supposed testament to failure. But delve deeper, and you'll find a narrative of trust, a sacred confidence that he, too, could flourish.

This tale is an echo of our own lives—how often have we viewed our 'one talent' as a limitation rather than a seed of potential? How frequently has fear rooted us in place, causing us to bury our gifts instead of investing them? This book challenges these fears, urging a reclamation of the talents we've been given, to invest them, not in the soil of dread, but in the fertile ground of faith and possibility.

Each chapter of this book is a step on the path of transforming inaction into action, fear into courage. Through reflective questions and the invitation to introspection, we will not only study but live this parable, allowing it to mirror our lives and guide us to a life of purpose, faith, and courage.

As we stand at the precipice of this journey, remember that the "one talent man" is more than a cautionary tale—he is a beacon of hope, a call to dig deep within ourselves, to confront our buried potential, and to rise above fear. Let us embrace this challenge, not as a burden, but as a gift—a chance to discover the fullness of our potential and to step into the adventure that life truly is.

So, with hearts open to the transformative power of God's word, let's embark on this journey together. Let's dig up the buried talents within ourselves and step into the abundant life promised to those who invest their gifts wisely. The journey begins now, and its path is yours to shape. Welcome to "The One Talent Challenge."

Tony Lee

The Parable of the Talents – Matthew 25: 14-30

[14] "For *the kingdom of heaven is* like a man traveling to a far country, *who* called his own servants and delivered his goods to them. [15] And to one he gave five talents, to another two, and to another one, to each according to his own ability; and immediately he went on a journey. [16] Then he who had received the five talents went and traded with them, and made another five talents. [17] And likewise he who *had received* two gained two more also. [18] But he who had received one went and dug in the ground, and hid his lord's money. [19] After a long time the lord of those servants came and settled accounts with them.

[20] "So he who had received five talents came and brought five other talents, saying, 'Lord, you delivered to me five talents; look, I have gained five more talents besides them.' [21] His lord said to him, 'Well *done,* good and faithful servant; you were faithful over a few things, I will make you ruler over many things. Enter into the joy of your lord.' [22] He also who had received two talents came and said, 'Lord, you delivered to me two talents; look, I have gained two more talents besides them.' [23] His lord said to him, 'Well *done,* good and faithful servant; you have been faithful over a few things, I will make you ruler over many things. Enter into the joy of your lord.'

[24] "Then he who had received the one talent came and said, 'Lord, I knew you to be a hard man, reaping where you have not sown, and gathering where you have not scattered seed. [25] And I was afraid, and went and hid your talent in the ground. Look, *there* you have *what is* yours.'

[26] "But his lord answered and said to him, 'You wicked and lazy servant, you knew that I reap where I have not sown, and gather where I have not scattered seed. [27] So you ought to have deposited my money with the bankers, and at my coming I would have received back my own with interest. [28] So take the talent from him, and give *it* to him who has ten talents.

[29] 'For to everyone who has, more will be given, and he will have abundance; but from him who does not have, even what he has will be taken away. [30] And cast the unprofitable servant into the outer darkness. There will be weeping and gnashing of teeth.'

CHAPTER 1

THE GIFT OF TRUST

"The most common way people give up their power is by thinking they don't have any."

– ALICE WALKER

In the serene landscapes of the heart, where the soil of our souls is both tilled and tested, there lies a profound narrative—a parable spoken by Jesus, known as the Parable of the Talents. Within the Gospel of Matthew (25:14-30), this story is a timeless treasure, offering layers of wisdom for those who seek to unearth its riches. This chapter is an invitation to delve into the narrative of the "one talent man," to discern the quiet whispers of truth that resonate as loudly today as they did two millennia ago.

The Master of the estate, emblematic of God, distributed talents among His servants according to their abilities. To one, He gave five talents; to another, two; and to another, one. This distribution was not random but was a deliberate act of trust, a divine investment into the lives of those He created. The gift was not merely monetary—it was an opportunity, a mission, a slice of the Master's own kingdom entrusted to human hands.

The focus of our reflection lies with the "one talent man," whose story often garners a shadow of negativity in today's success-driven culture. Society may label him as underachieving, his single talent a mark of mediocrity. Yet, there is an untold narrative of trust that we must excavate. For the Master to entrust him with a talent indicates a sacred confidence, a belief that this servant had the capacity to flourish. It is an affirmation often overlooked, clouded by the eventual outcome of the story.

This man, given one talent, stood upon a foundation of trust—trust that was perhaps built upon years of toil, loyalty, and previous successes. He was not an outsider but a member of the household, likely esteemed by his peers, for he bore a portion of the Master's wealth. His history of production, the fruits of his labor that we do not see, warranted the Master's decision to entrust him with this treasure.

God's entrustment of talents to each individual is a profound expression of divine trust and belief in our potential. In bestowing us with unique gifts and abilities, God is not only recognizing our inherent value but is also inviting us to participate in the larger tapestry of creation and purpose. These talents, whether they are artistic abilities, intellectual capacities, spiritual insights, or acts of service, are not given arbitrarily; they are carefully apportioned in alignment with our unique personalities and life paths.

This divine trust is a call to action, an encouragement to cultivate and utilize these gifts not just for our own fulfillment, but as a means of contributing to the greater good and manifesting God's love in the world. The distribution of these talents is a testament to God's wisdom in knowing what we are capable of, even if we sometimes doubt our own abilities. It's a reminder that each of us has a role to play, a unique contribution to make, and that in doing so, we not only honor our Creator, but we also discover deeper layers of our own identity and purpose. In trusting us with these talents, God is essentially inviting us into a partnership, a co-creation where our personal growth and spiritual journey contribute to the unfolding of a larger, divine plan.

However, trust is but the first step in the dance of stewardship. It is an invitation to partnership, to enter into the work of the kingdom with creativity and courage. The Master's trust is a silent plea, a call to action that resounds in the depths of the "one talent man's" being. It is the starting line of a race meant to be run, a venture of faith that beckons beyond the safety of the familiar.

As we stand in the shoes of the "one talent man," we are compelled to ask ourselves: How do we respond to the trust that has been placed in us? Do we see our one talent as a limitation or as a seed of potential awaiting cultivation? The answers to these questions are not found in the echoes of societal expectations but in the intimate chambers where our hearts commune with the Divine.

Reflection Questions:

1. Reflect on a time when you were entrusted with a responsibility. How did it make you feel about your capabilities?
2. In what ways can society's view of success impact our understanding of what it means to be faithful with what we have been given?
3. How can we identify and combat the fear that may prevent us from utilizing the talents we've been entrusted with?
4. Consider the talents and gifts you possess. How are you currently using them to produce fruit in your life and the lives of others?
5. The "one talent man" had a history with the Master. Reflect on your history with God. How has He prepared you for the responsibilities He has entrusted to you?

CHAPTER 2

THE TALENT GRAVEYARD

"There is only one thing that makes a dream impossible to achieve: the fear of failure."

– PAULO COELHO

Beneath the tranquil surface of trust, where Chapter One led us to ponder the sacred confidence bestowed upon the "one talent man," there lies a darker stratum that Chapter Two dares to excavate—the Talent Graveyard. Here, talents lie dormant, shrouded not in soil but in the heavy cloak of anxiety and fear. It is a place where potential is entombed, and opportunity is obscured by the looming shadows of "what if."

The concept of a talent graveyard conjures a poignant and powerful image, a metaphorical landscape where unrealized potential and unexpressed gifts lie dormant. It's a silent expanse filled with dreams unchased, ideas unexpressed, and abilities untapped, each one a monument to what could have been. This graveyard represents the culmination of fears, doubts, and insecurities that have led individuals to bury their innate talents, often without realizing the extent of their loss. It's a space where opportunities for joy, innovation, and contribution to the world have been obscured by the shadows of what-ifs and regrets.

Each buried talent in this graveyard holds a story, a narrative of a path not taken, a risk not ventured, or a voice silenced by the harsh judgments of self or others. The talent graveyard serves as a stark reminder of the importance of nurturing and expressing our talents, encouraging us not to let our potential wither away unexplored.

Anxiety whispers insidiously, a serpent coiling around the heart, squeezing with questions of worthiness and capability. "Am I able?" it hisses. "What will happen if I fail?" The "one talent man" stood at this precipice, the weight of the talent in his hands matched by the burden of these silent queries. Anxiety, a thief of joy, can paralyze the spirit, turning the gift of a talent into a stone too heavy to lift.

Fear, too, plays its part—a cruel jailer that confines us within walls of inaction. It is a potent force that can arrest the hand poised to create, to invest, to risk. The "one talent man" may have peered into the future and seen the peril of loss greater than the promise of gain. Inaction, then, became his refuge, a place of seeming safety where nothing is risked but everything is lost.

The Biblical perspective on fear is clear: it is not the fabric of which faith is woven. Scripture resonates with the refrain "Do not be afraid," a command that echoes through the ages, finding its way to our hearts today. The Christian response to fear is trust—not in our own power, but in the One who has given the talent. It is a trust that acknowledges our limitations but leans on the limitless nature of God.

The Master, who represents God, understands our frame, knows the dust from which we are formed, and yet calls us to rise above our fears. The talent is not merely an investment; it is a test and a testament to His belief in our potential. The "one talent man" was not condemned for his lack of success but for his unwillingness to try, for burying his talent in the graveyard of his fears rather than planting it in the faith-filled soil of possibility.

As we journey through the Talent Graveyard, let us be mindful that the same choice presented to the "one talent man" is ours to make. Will we let fear dictate our actions, or will we embrace the risk inherent in faith? Our talents, whether they seem like one or many, are not just for our own development but are entrusted to us for the growth of the kingdom.

Reflection Questions:

1. Recall a time when fear influenced your decision. What was the outcome, and what did you learn from the experience?
2. How does the biblical command to "fear not" challenge the way you approach the talents and opportunities God has given you?
3. Reflect on the parable's "one talent man." How does understanding his fear change your perspective on his actions and your own?
4. Consider ways in which you may have buried your talents out of fear. What steps can you take to unearth and invest them now?
5. Contemplate the relationship between fear and faith in your life. How can strengthening your faith help you overcome your fears?

CHAPTER 3

Trauma and Talents

"When we are no longer able to change a situation, we are challenged to change ourselves."

– Victor Frankl

In the dimly lit corridors of the human experience, trauma often acts as a silent sentinel, guarding the gates where our talents are meant to flourish. The parable of the talents, as narrated in Matthew 25:14-30, not only speaks of stewardship and diligence but also touches on the profound impact of our inner turmoil on the external manifestation of our gifts. This chapter delves into the complex relationship between personal trauma and the burying of our talents.

Previous seasons of hardship etch deep grooves into the soul's terrain, and these grooves can direct the flow of our productivity. It is not uncommon for the challenges of the past to cast long shadows over our current endeavors, influencing how we engage with the talents entrusted to us. Trauma, with its insidious tendrils, can cause a cascade of issues—be it anxiety, health complications, financial instability, relational strain, or the myriad disappointments that life hurls our way. These are the unseen battles that wage war against our potential.

The "one talent man" might have been a casualty of such

struggles, his decision to bury his talent a manifestation of deeper wounds. Perhaps the fear that immobilized him was borne of trauma—a visceral reaction to the possibility of failure that overwhelmed his capacity to act. In understanding this, we approach his story not with judgment, but with empathy, recognizing the shared human condition that often wrestles with the paralysis of fear.

Trauma can profoundly impact our psyche, often leading us to bury our talents as a form of self-preservation. In the wake of traumatic experiences, the world can seem more threatening, and our vulnerabilities feel more exposed. This heightened sense of vulnerability can cause us to recoil and hide those parts of ourselves that we perceive as most susceptible to harm, including our unique talents and abilities.

These talents, often deeply intertwined with our sense of identity and self-expression, can become casualties in our attempt to protect ourselves from further pain. The fear of judgment, criticism, or failure, all amplified by past trauma, can lead to a self-imposed isolation of our abilities. The process of burying our talents in response to trauma is a survival mechanism, an unconscious effort to erect barriers against perceived threats. However, in doing so, we inadvertently limit our potential and deny ourselves the opportunity for healing and growth that comes from engaging with and sharing our inherent gifts. This retreat into the shadows, while initially a refuge, can ultimately become a prison, holding us back from fully experiencing life and realizing our true potential.

Healing from trauma is akin to reclaiming sunken treasures; it is a journey that requires courage, persistence, and often, guidance. Coping mechanisms—ranging from seeking support, engaging in reflective practices, embracing creativity, to pursuing professional help—are like tools that aid in the excavation of buried talents. The healing process, though unique to each individual, often involves confronting the pain, understanding its origins, and gradually learning to navigate life with newfound resilience.

As one learns to reclaim their talents, they are often surprised to find that their gifts have not diminished but rather lay dormant, waiting to be unearthed. The act of bringing them to light can be a cathartic experience, one that not only contributes to personal growth but also serves as a testament to overcoming adversity.

It is important to explore strategies to unearth and cultivate our God-given talents, even as we navigate the complexities of our traumas. It is a call to action, to rise from the ashes of our experiences, armed with the knowledge that our talents are not only meant for personal fulfillment but also as a conduit for divine purpose.

Reflection Questions:

1. Reflect on a personal trauma that may have contributed to the burying of your talents. How has it shaped your actions?
2. In what ways can you identify coping mechanisms that have been helpful or detrimental to your talent cultivation?
3. Consider the healing processes that resonate with you. How can you implement these to help reclaim your buried talents?
4. How does the story of the "one talent man" inspire you to address your own traumas and to activate the talents you possess?
5. Meditate on the relationship between healing from trauma and stewardship of talents. How can embracing one aid in fulfilling the other?

CHAPTER 4

THE SEASONAL NATURE OF TALENTS

*"The only person you are destined to become
is the person you decide to be."*

— RALPH WALDO EMERSON

In the tapestry of life, every thread has its hue, every season its own unique pattern of light and shade. Similarly, our talents, those individual gifts granted by the divine, ebb and flow with the seasons of our existence. The parable of the talents, a mere snapshot within the continuum of life's grand narrative, captures this very essence—the seasonal nature of our abilities and resources.

At one juncture, the characters of the parable who handled five and three talents might have navigated seasons where managing even one was all they could muster. Like trees stripped bare in winter, only to burgeon with foliage in spring, our capacity to handle talents can be subject to the vicissitudes of life's seasons. In seasons of abundance, our branches hang heavy with fruit; in times of scarcity, we may find ourselves bare, with seemingly little to offer.

The seasonal nature of talents reflects the dynamic and ever-evolving journey of our lives, where the different seasons bring varying conditions under which our talents can either flourish or lie dormant. Just as spring symbolizes growth and renewal, there are periods in our lives where our talents naturally blossom, fueled by the right circumstances, experiences, and personal readiness.

These are times of vibrant expression and discovery, where our abilities align seamlessly with the opportunities at hand. Conversely, in the autumnal phases of life, certain talents might recede, much like leaves falling from trees, making way for a different set of skills or interests to take root. Winter, often characterized by introspection and stillness, might see some talents lying dormant, not because they are lost, but because they are in a state of rest and conservation, awaiting the next cycle of growth.

This seasonal perspective is crucial in understanding that not all talents are meant to be constantly in the forefront. Some abilities emerge strongly at specific points in our lives, while others might retreat temporarily, only to reemerge later with renewed vigor. This ebb and flow are natural and necessary, reminding us that our personal growth and expression of talents are not linear but cyclical, deeply influenced by the ever-changing seasons of our lives. Accepting this seasonal nature allows us to be more patient and forgiving with ourselves, understanding that each talent has its own time to shine.

This section weaves together stories of those who have traversed both the "five talent" and "one talent" seasons, testimonies that speak of the resilience and adaptability of the human spirit.

Take, for instance, Sarah, whose early years were marked by a vibrant creativity that led her to found a successful design company. Yet, a season of loss and grief saw her retreat, her once plentiful talents seemingly buried under the weight of sorrow. Or consider Michael, whose career was on a meteoric rise until a health crisis left him reassessing his life's work, confronted with the reality of a season of recovery and limitation.

These are not tales of linear progression but of the cyclical nature of growth and change. They serve as a reminder that a season of "one talent" is not a sentence to inactivity but a period of conservation and potential reorientation. It is in these times that the groundwork is laid for future abundance, where the lessons learned in scarcity can enrich the times of plenty.

Moreover, these seasonal shifts invite a deeper understanding of stewardship. Just as a skilled gardener knows when to prune and when to plant, we too are called to discern the seasons of our talents. There are times for bold investment and times for careful conservation, times to step forward and times to reflect and heal.

As these stories unfold, we witness the transformative power of faith and perseverance. Sarah's journey leads her to rediscover her creative spark in mentoring others, while Michael finds new purpose in advocating for health awareness. Their seasons of "one talent" did not denote the end but rather served as a chrysalis from which new forms of talent emerged, reshaped and repurposed for the path ahead.

Tony Lee

In contemplating the seasonal nature of our talents, we find solace in the knowledge that no season is permanent, and each has its purpose under heaven. We learn to navigate these shifts with grace, understanding that our talents are not static endowments but dynamic gifts, ever-changing with the seasons of our lives.

Reflection Questions:

1. Can you identify the current season of your life regarding your talents? Are you in a season of growth, conservation, or transition?
2. Recall a time when you felt like a "one talent" individual. What did that season teach you about yourself and your capabilities?
3. How can recognizing the seasonal nature of your talents alter the way you approach your goals and steward your gifts?
4. Reflect on the lives of Sarah and Michael. How do their stories inspire you to adapt to the changing seasons of your own talents?
5. Contemplate the ways in which you can prepare for future seasons of abundance during a current season of conservation or scarcity.

CHAPTER 5

SERMONS IN THE SOIL

"It is impossible to live without failing at something, unless you live so cautiously that you might as well not have lived at all - in which case, you fail by default."

— J.K. ROWLING

The gifts we have buried, our "sermons in the soil," are poignant reminders of the potential that lies dormant within us, awaiting our courage to unearth them. These buried talents are not just lost opportunities, but they are also profound teachers in their own right. They teach us about the nature of fear and the cost of yielding to it. As we contemplate the skills, dreams, and passions we have hidden away, we learn about the parts of ourselves that we have neglected or undervalued.

These buried gifts challenge us to confront our fears and insecurities, pushing us to grow beyond the confines of our comfort zones. The act of uncovering these talents is transformative, not only in harnessing these abilities but also in the process of self-discovery and empowerment it entails. Each unburied gift is a testament to our resilience and an invitation to live a life more fully realized. In essence, our buried gifts, once unearthed, become powerful tools in sculpting a more authentic and fulfilling life, teaching us the invaluable lesson that what we fear to confront might just be what holds the key to our greatest growth and fulfillment.

This chapter delves into the pivotal moment of the parable—the reckoning of the servant who buried his talent. It is a moment that transcends time and place, resonating with anyone who has ever grappled with the fear of failure or the paralysis of uncertainty. Here, we explore the inner journey of the "one talent" servant, peeling back the layers of his decision to bury his gift.

The story of this servant is a metaphor for the self-imposed limitations we often place on our potential. This man's action, driven by fear, is a mirror reflecting our own tendencies to shrink back when confronted with opportunities that demand risk and faith. The act of burying, in many ways, is an act of self-preservation, a shield against the possibility of failure and the sting of rejection.

We must begin to explore the internal struggle of the servant, a struggle that resonates deeply with many of us. What was the root of his fear? Was it solely the dread of his master's reaction, or was it something more profound – a fear of failure, of not meeting expectations, or of stepping into the unfamiliar? In dissecting these fears, we find insights into our own insecurities and hesitations. The act of burying the talent is symbolic of how we often respond to fear – by retreating into our comfort zones, avoiding risks, and thus inadvertently stifling our growth and development. This behavior is not just about the loss of potential gains but also about the loss of self-discovery and the joy of contributing our unique gifts to the world.

This narrative takes us beyond the biblical context, presenting the parable as a timeless allegory of human potential and the transformative power of facing and overcoming fear. It urges readers to challenge the constraints fear imposes, encouraging them to bravely utilize their talents for their own fulfillment and for the greater good.

This chapter's reflective questions, invite you to engage in personal introspection. These questions are designed to guide you through a process of recognizing where you might have 'buried your talents' due to fear. It encourages you to consider how the fear of failure or judgment has impacted your willingness to use your talents and how confronting these fears can lead to personal growth and self-discovery.

Reflection Questions:

1. Reflect on a talent or passion you have neglected or buried. What fears or doubts have held you back from fully embracing this part of yourself?
2. How does the fear of failure or judgment affect your willingness to use your talents?
3. In what ways can confronting and understanding your fears lead to personal growth and self-discovery?
4. Imagine the potential impact on your life and the lives of those around you if you were to fully utilize your buried talents. What does this vision inspire in you?

CHAPTER 6

Dig It Up

"It is never too late to be what you might have been."

– George Eliot

As the dawn of each day heralds new beginnings, so does each chapter of our lives present fresh opportunities to unearth the talents we've buried. The parable of the talents, particularly the tale of the one-talent man, is not merely a cautionary story but also a beacon of hope for second chances.

The master's extended journey can be seen as a grace period granted to us—a time to toil, reflect, and ultimately, act upon the talents we've hidden away. It's a metaphor for the life we are given, the stretch of years filled with moments where we can choose to either dig up or bury deeper the abilities that define us.

In this interim, while the master is away, the world does not stand still, and neither should we. The fields in which we can sow our talents are vast, and the time to till them is now. It is a profound truth that as long as life endures, the hands of the clock never cease their round, offering us endless moments to start anew.

Digging up talents we have buried is a transformative process, akin to unearthing hidden treasures long forgotten. It's an act of courage and self-reclamation, where we delve into the depths of our being to retrieve parts of ourselves left unattended. This journey often begins with introspection, a willingness to confront the fears and insecurities that led us to bury these talents in the first place. It requires honesty and vulnerability, as we acknowledge the potential we have ignored or suppressed due to various life circumstances or self-doubt.

The act of unearthing these buried talents is not just about rediscovery, but also about reintegration - weaving these talents back into the fabric of our lives, allowing them to add color, depth, and texture to our existence. This process can be challenging, as it may involve breaking through layers of resistance, but it is incredibly rewarding. It leads to a renewal of self-confidence and purpose, as we begin to recognize and embrace the full spectrum of our abilities. As these talents resurface, they bring with them new opportunities for growth, expression, and fulfillment. In digging up what we once buried, we open ourselves up to new possibilities and a deeper understanding of our true potential.

So, what have you buried? A dream? A skill? A passion, perhaps, that you've deemed too insignificant to pursue? It's time to dig it up. Each talent, no matter how small it appears, holds the potential for greatness. The one-talent man's failure was not in the talent itself but in his decision to bury it. Your talent, when invested, can yield a harvest beyond what you can imagine.

Let us take a shovel to the hard soil of our fears and doubts, and excavate the talents we've entombed. It may require effort; the ground may be unyielding at first, but the act of digging is in itself an investment. With each shovelful of earth, we move closer to bringing our talents into the light where they belong.

Remember, the master's return is certain, but the time is not. The period of waiting is not a pause but a time for preparation, for work, for growth. It is a gift, though it may not seem so, for in the waiting we find the strength and resolve to do what must be done.

We are called not to linger on what has been but to focus on what can be. The past is etched in stone, but the future is clay, waiting to be shaped by the choices we make today. So let us choose to dig up our talents, to invest them wisely, and to watch them grow, for as long as life endures, it's never too late to begin again.

Reflection Questions:

1. What is the one talent you have buried, and what has prevented you from investing it?
2. How can the understanding that life is a grace period change the way you approach your talents?
3. What practical steps can you take today to begin unearthing and nurturing your buried talents?
4. How does the concept of time as a resource affect your perspective on personal growth and talent development?
5. Envision the one-talent man taking a different path. What would he do upon realizing his error, and how can his hypothetical journey inspire your own?

Conclusion

*"We may encounter many defeats but
we must not be defeated."*

– **Maya Angelou**

In our journey through "**The One Talent Challenge: Overcoming Inaction and Fear**," we have delved into the rich soil of self-discovery, exploring the depths of trust, confronting the shadows of fear, and witnessing the redemptive power that even the smallest talent holds when it is courageously invested. The parable from Matthew 25:14-30 serves as more than an ancient narrative; it is a mirror reflecting the hidden parts of our own lives, revealing the treasures we've buried—sometimes knowingly, other times unknowingly—underneath the weight of self-doubt and complacency.

We have walked alongside the one-talent man, peered into his heart, and seen our own reflections. His story, a blend of regret and caution, ends with a talent still buried, a potential untapped. Yet, his ending does not have to be ours. Our chapters are still being written, and within them lies the chance for a different choice, a brave step towards redemption.

This concluding chapter is not the end but a beginning—a call to action for each of us. A summons to no longer walk past the mounds of earth under which our talents lie dormant. It's a charge to pick up the spade of determination and dig up the gifts we've been given, to invest them in the service of others, and in doing so, enrich our own lives and the world around us.

The fear that once whispered that our talents were too insignificant to matter has been exposed as a lie. The truth is, every talent has the power to ignite change, to create, to heal, and to inspire. It is in the wielding of our talents that we become who we were meant to be, not only for our own sake but for the sake of those who will be touched by what we bring forth from the ground.

Therefore, let this book not merely rest on your shelf, but let it rest in your heart as a reminder that the time to act is now. Embrace the grace period life offers, and let it not pass by unheeded. Let the ticking of the clock not be a countdown to regret but a rhythm to which you step forward into growth, into action, into a life of meaningful contribution.

The world awaits the fruits of your talents. May you dig them up, may you invest them wisely, and may you reap a harvest that surpasses your wildest dreams. Your story is still unfolding, and in it, there is much to be written. So rise, dig up your talent, and step into the fullness of your potential. The time is now, and it is yours.

www.ingramcontent.com/pod-product-compliance
Lightning Source LLC
Chambersburg PA
CBHW071800040426
42446CB00012B/2640